No part of this publication may be reproduced, stored in a retrieval system or transmitted in any form or by any means, electronic, mechanical, photocopying, recording, or otherwise, without express written permission of the author.

"Jesus Has an Awesome Fun Life for Me!"
Dr. Patricia Brown

Illustrated by: Jacqi Smith

©Copyright 2020 All rights reserved

ISBN 978-0-9859551-1-3

Published by:
Publish Affordably.com
Chicago, Illinois • 773-783-2981

DEDICATION

First of all, I dedicate this series to the Holy Spirit because without His help, guidance and encouragement, this work would have been impossible.

I also dedicate this to my awesome, loving children, Alison and Stephen and to my amazing Aunt Daisy, whom I love dearly.

Acknowledgments

I want to thank my phenomenal pastors, Pastors Stephen and Candy LaFlora. Your love, patience, teaching and support are vital ingredients that helped to catapult me to a place where I can confidently fulfill my purpose, which is making Jesus cool to kids. Words alone cannot express how much I love and appreciate both of you. From the deepest recesses of my heart, I say God bless you!

I am grateful for my friend and sister in Christ, Melissa Duff Brown. Melissa, you are an amazing, brilliant woman of God whose knowledge, wisdom and array of talents have helped to guide me. I am so blessed to be able to call you my friend!

I am thankful for my mentors in children's ministry, Pastor Marla Hines and Jojo Bioh. These strong women of God helped to shape me, and from each, I have learned keys to ministry that I deeply treasure and for which I will be eternally grateful.

I express gratitude to Sister Sarah LaFlora for being an example of a virtuous, godly, wise woman to me and to the body of Christ.

Last, but certainly not least, I am grateful to my cousin Tamela Douglas, who loved and supported me during one of the darkest periods of my life. Without her help, I would not have been able to continue with this project. Tami, thank you, and I will always love you!

Preface

Jesus Has an Awesome, Fun Life for Me! is a series written for the next generation of the body of Christ. I accepted Jesus as my Lord and Savior when I was eight, and as a result of that decision, I knew I would go to heaven when I died. I thank God that I had a prayerful mother who taught me from a young age that God loves me, and that reassured me that He has a good plan for my life.

Growing up in the church, I saw so many saints suffer sickness, poverty, and misery; I heard them frequently refer to the wonderful life they would experience once they got to heaven as they lived in a continuous state of dejection and insufficiency.

After I completed college and postgraduate training, my income increased beyond my wildest dreams. While I was grateful to God, after a while I began to feel uneasy about my success because I continued to see my fellow Christians struggle. Of course, I helped many, but there was only so much one person could do (there is a God, but His name is not Pat!).

I began to ask serious questions about why I was so blessed while my brothers and sisters in Christ were in such dire straits.

I knew that God is no respecter of persons, and that the Word said that those who hunger and thirst after righteousness will be filled.

I was confident in God's love for me and His desire to broaden my understanding about why I was blessed and so many others were not (or so it seemed).

The truth is that all believers have access to an abundant and fulfilled life. I currently teach in children's ministry; I love the children as if they're my own, and I want to see them do well. We as teachers want our children to benefit from our experiences without having to make the same mistakes we did. I want these young believers to grow up knowing the rich heritage that's theirs because of what Jesus did for them on the cross. I want them to learn early how to tap into and experience what's available to them at a young age, and then take that knowledge to the next level and use it to build the kingdom of God. They can live well here on earth while remembering that they're blessed to be a blessing. I want learning about their heritage to be fun for the children.

To this end, I've devoted a short book to each of the finished works of Jesus in which I endeavor to make learning about our inheritance easy and enjoyable. Revelation 5:12 (KJV) is referenced: "Worthy is the Lamb that was slain to receive power, and riches, and wisdom, and strength, and honor, and glory, and blessing." Thank you for joining me on this journey!

Dr. Pat Brown

Jesus Has an Awesome, Fun Life for You!

Mom

Justine

Chris

Ms Joanne

Josh

Rachel

Angel

Mark

Annie

"Good morning, kids! It's time to wake up and get ready for church."

"Good morning, Mom!"

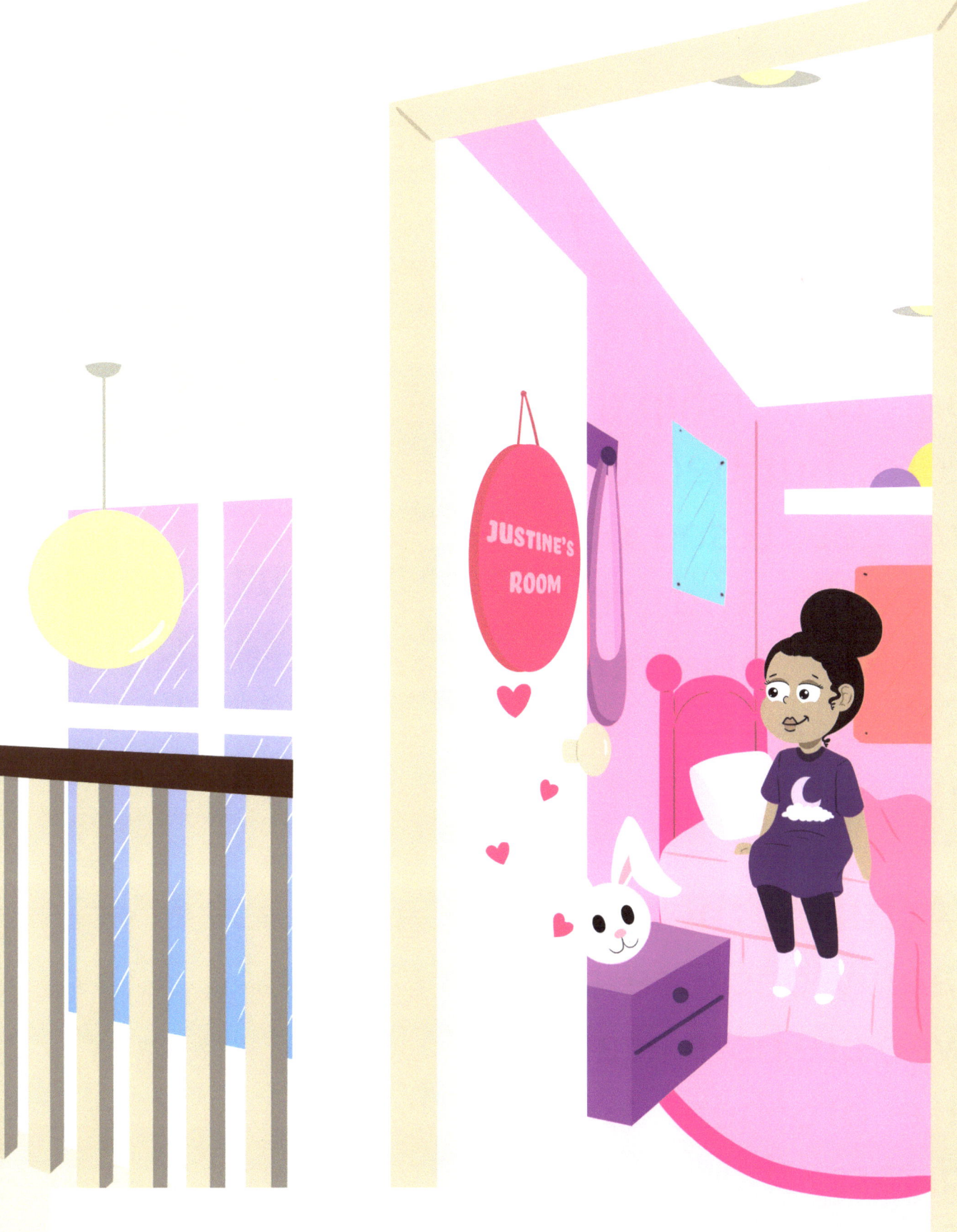

"Hi, Mom!"

"I'm really excited because it's Sunday. I look forward to going to church not only to worship the Lord, but because we get to see our friends and the other Christians because they are like family.

"Actually, they are family because all who are born again are brothers and sisters, children of God. Jesus is our oldest brother."

"I like going to church because I get to go to children's church. They talk about Jesus and the Bible so I can understand it.

"I get to hang out with my friends, and we get to sing and play fun games."

"I like it too! Sometimes when we play games, if we answer a question right, we get to pick out prizes. Last Sunday, I got a new dress for my doll!"

Chris and Justine hurry to get ready and eat breakfast. They want to get to church early so they'll have time to play with their friends before service starts.

Mom reminds them to feed their cat, Tony, before they leave.

"Traffic was light this morning. We got here pretty quick. Come on, guys; let's go inside!"

Mom checks the children in at the children's ministry desk. She gives both Chris and Justine a hug and gives them money for tithes and offerings.

"Bye, kids! I'll see you after service."

Chris and Justine go into their classroom, and as they had planned, they are early. Their friends Rachel and Mark are already there.

"Hey, Mark!"

"Hi, Chris! Want to play on the scooters? We have a few minutes before class starts."

"Justine, I found this really pretty doll in the toy box. Want to help me comb her hair?"

"Yeah! That would be fun!"

"Salvation is when I ask Jesus to forgive me for my sins, and I ask Him to save me so that when I die, I will go to heaven."

"That's right Chris; good answer. But there's so much more that comes with salvation. Really, we can think of salvation as a package that has a lot of parts," said Ms. Joanne."

"What do you mean?" asked Rachael.

"Yeah, what's that supposed to mean?" Angel replied.

Ms. Joanne continued, "Well, Jesus died and rose on the third day. Revelation 5:12 (KJV) says, "Worthy is the Lamb [meaning Jesus] that was slain to receive power, and riches, and wisdom, and strength, and honor, and glory, and blessing!"

"Today we'll focus on power, and over the next several weeks, we'll spend time understanding each thing that Jesus got for us."

"Can someone tell me what power is?"

"Power means you're strong and you can win fights."

"I mean, he's not wrong . . ." Angel said.

Ms. Joanne replied, "Well, Chris, that's partly right."

"See?" Angel said.

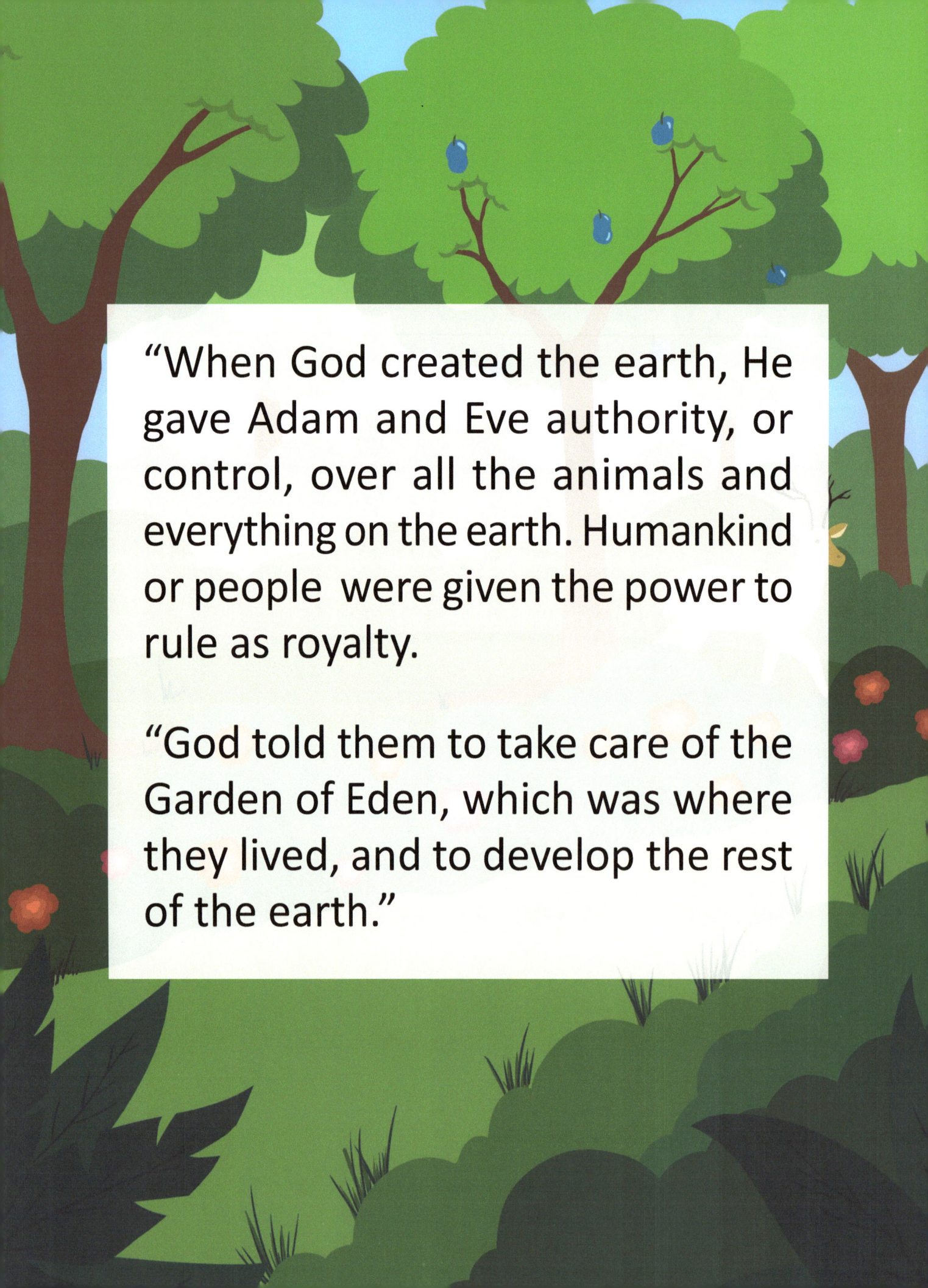

"When God created the earth, He gave Adam and Eve authority, or control, over all the animals and everything on the earth. Humankind or people were given the power to rule as royalty.

"God told them to take care of the Garden of Eden, which was where they lived, and to develop the rest of the earth."

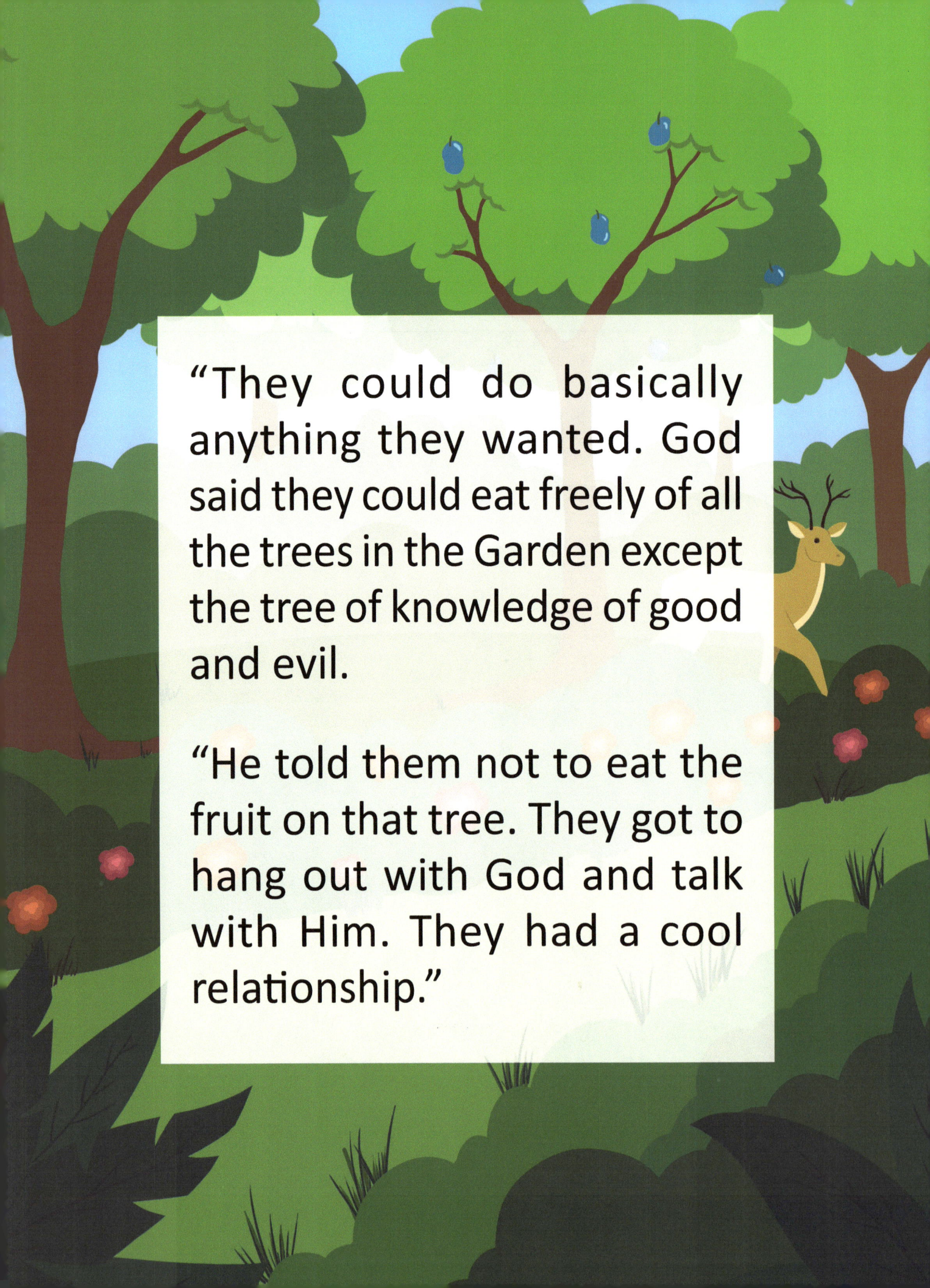

"They could do basically anything they wanted. God said they could eat freely of all the trees in the Garden except the tree of knowledge of good and evil.

"He told them not to eat the fruit on that tree. They got to hang out with God and talk with Him. They had a cool relationship."

"But when the humans sinned by disobeying God and ate the fruit from the tree that God told them not to, the curse came to the earth.

"The power that God had given us was lost to satan, who was talking through the serpent."

"Adam and Eve were put out of the Garden. They no longer had control of the beautiful place God had made for them. They no longer had the power to rule the earth.

"People were now in a terrible condition. God loved them so much, and it really hurt God that he couldn't have the same kind of relationship with the people on the earth.

"He really wanted a family, and He had made humans so he could have that family."

John 3:16-17

"For *God* so *Loved* the *world*, that he *gave* his only begotten *Son*, that whosoever *believeth* in *Him* should not *perish*, but have *everlasting life*.

"For *God* sent not his *Son* into the *world* to condemn the world; but that the world through *Him* might be *Saved*."

"When a man, woman, boy, or girl accepts Jesus as their savior, Jesus comes to live inside their spirit."

"Because Jesus took back the power, when we accept Jesus, we have the same power that He has."

"When we're born again, Jesus can use us to perform miracles."

Ms. Joanne continued, "We'll speak in a new language, a heavenly language, which is the baptism of the Holy Spirit.

Baptism with the Holy Spirit gives us access to the most powerful force on the planet!"

"Even a child who accepts Jesus can lay hands on a sick person and pray in the name of Jesus, and they will be healed just like Jesus did when He was here on earth."

"Boys and girls, what Jesus did for us is just awesome! He is our hero, Lord, and Savior!"

"Today we only covered the first of the seven things that Jesus came to take back for us. Next week, we'll talk about riches."

"Before we end class today, would anyone like to accept Jesus as their savior?"

Ms. Joanne continues, "Please repeat after me, and the boys and girls reading can repeat after me, too!"

"Lord Jesus, I believe You're the son of God; You died and rose again on the third day. I ask You to forgive me for my sins and I accept You as my savior.

"Raise your hand if you just accepted Jesus."

"This is a very exciting day! If you said the prayer for the first time, the angels are rejoicing, and your name is recorded in the Book of Life in heaven."

ABOUT THE AUTHOR

Patricia Brown, M.D. was born again when she was eight; she teaches in children's ministry and has a passion for making Jesus cool to kids. She is the mother of talented teenage twins.

Upon completion of her training at the University of Chicago, Dr. Pat practiced pediatrics for several years. She currently has a fulfilling nonclinical medicine practice which allows her to use her medical knowledge and her gift of writing.

www.ingramcontent.com/pod-product-compliance
Lightning Source LLC
LaVergne TN
LVHW072113070426
835510LV00002B/25